# THE BOOK OF BLESSINGS

© Photographer: Melissa Schalke

BY JACKY SACHS

Kennebunkport, Maine

13 Digit ISBN: 978-1-933662-33-6
10 Digit ISBN: 1-933662-33-6

This book may be ordered by mail from the publisher.
Please include $3.50 for postage and handling.

Please support your local bookseller first!

Books published by Cider mill Press Book Publishers are available at special discounts for bulk purchases in the United States by corporations, institutions, and other organizations. For more information, please contact the publisher.
Cider Mill Press Book Publishers

"Where good books are ready for press"
12 Port Farm Road
Kennebunkport, Maine 04046

Visit us on the web!
www.cidermillpress.com

Design by: neo9 design inc.
Typography: Apollo, Herculanum

Printed in China
1 2 3 4 5 6 7 8 9 10
First Edition

# CONTENTS

## INTRODUCTION

# ONE WORLD

They are little squares of hope and good intention. Colorful flags that bounce on the wind, creating sacred spaces of harmony, reminding us to be mindful and aware as we go about our business of life. They are the prayer flags.

This book aims to teach you a little about these beautiful squares of prayer. You will learn their history, how to use them, and even how to make your own. There will be suggestions for your flags: whether for everyday usage, as gifts, or to mark special occasions, among others. You'll even find a chapter containing words of wisdom from around the world to help you create your own unique set of prayer flags, or generate your own mantras, prayers, and invocations. The box contains two sets of prayer flags. One set are the traditional flags, and the blank set is for you to decorate and bless, creating your own call for happiness, virtue, mindfulness, peace, and harmony in the world.

Prayer flags come to us from Tibet, a magical land nestled in the breathtakingly beautiful and snowy Himalayan range between China and India. When

we think of Tibet, we may think of the exiled Dalai Lama, one of the most amazing and respected men on Earth. We may conjure images of a country filled with sherpas, sari swathed monks, monasteries, mandalas, sand art, and woven scarves and hats. We are tantalized by the exotic food like yak butter and butter tea. We might think of Shangri-la, the "rooftop of the world," buddhas, mystics, mantras, walking barefoot in the snow, meditation, bodhisattvas, prayer wheels, thankgas, and the wonderfully colorful prayer flags blowing in the breeze. To visit the Himalayan mountain towns is to be transported to a truly remarkable world, and we've embraced everything we can soak up from this mystical culture.

© Photo by: Jason Maehl

Tibetan Buddhism and its symbols subsequently entered the consciousness of people all over the world as His Holiness, the 14th Dalai Lama, moved to educate the world about Tibet, peace, compassion, and a better way of life. And so it is that we find the blue, white, red, green, and yellow fabric squares of prayer flags fluttering in the breeze in our very own backyards, cafes, storefronts, fire escapes, gas stations, and dorm rooms, carrying our prayers into the mix. We are captivated by these little squares of peace and love and have adopted them as our own, hoping to bring some of the compassion and peace of their intention into our own small corner of the world. Hoping for some of the Dalai Lama's "happiness" secrets for ourselves and for our friends the world over. The magic of prayer flags lies in our intentions as we send them out on the wind to launch our hopes and dreams. Such wonderful intentions . . . blowing on the breeze.

## CHAPTER ONE

# MEET THE WIND HORSE

## THE HISTORY OF PRAYER FLAGS

The compassionate heart of the Buddhist religion has truly reached the four corners of our world. We see statuettes of buddhas and prayer flags in restaurants and shops, in urban cafes and country gardens. Even in the most remote, rural corners of many western countries one can find one's self surrounded by community food coops, thoroughbred farms, and surprisingly, prayer flags strung from maple trees and fence posts. So where did it all start?

Buddhism traces its roots back to the son of a chief and king in the Shakyamuni region on the border of northern India and southern Nepal, nestled in the Himalayan foothills. His name was Siddhartha, which means "every wish fulfilled."

© Photo by: Jason Maehl

# BOY MEETS BUDDHA

© Photo by: Hans Slegers

Siddhartha left the endless comforts of his royal home in search of a new way of life. He had seen the existence of suffering around him in every direction, and he vowed to end it, to awaken to a different way of life. And so legend has it that Siddhartha Guatama, after years of spiritual seeking, eventually found himself at the base of a bodhi tree, where he sat in meditation for six long years. As he sat he found his heart opening to a joy and love beyond his wildest expectation, and he inevitably experienced an enlightened state of mind and spirit. He had discovered the cessation of suffering with the awakening of the most tender of hearts, and vowed to teach others to follow the path he had taken so that they too could experience a life without suffering. He had become the Buddha, which means "he who is awake."

## ON THE PATH

The Buddha set forth to teach and so Buddhism spread. It spread throughout India to Sri Lanka, Burma, Thailand, Cambodia, Laos, and Indonesia. It flowed northward, to China and Japan. In the eighth century, it reached Tibet through a Buddhist monk named Padma Sambhava. The native religion in Tibet at this time was Bön, a shamanistic religion based on the concept of a world pervaded by good and evil spirits. Bön practices included rites, predictions, sacrifice, and sorcery.

At the heart of Bön was a belief that all things were interdependent: the ground and the sky, animals and humans, plants and rocks, oceans and deserts. Bön priests were largely concerned with taking care of the dead through ceremonies intended to ensure their safe journey to the afterlife and, much like the ancient Egyptians, ensure material prosperity once the other side was reached. These rituals often involved sacrifice of animals and offerings of gifts for the afterlife, including valuables such as jewels. Tibetans believed in gods who inhabited space from the underworld to the heavens. Deities were to be found everywhere in the natural world surrounding them.

Tibetans merged aspects of Bön into Buddhism, thus Tibetan Buddhism became a distinctive form of the practice like no other in the world, run through with magical and mystical elements.

## IN THE BEGINNING

© Photo by: Marcus Brown

Prayer flags are thought to have originated thousands of years ago in ancient Tibet for use during times of war. The prayers and mantras appearing on the flags acted as talismans to keep loss and suffering at bay. They protected the people against defeat at the hands of their enemies. They were eventually adapted into the Bön culture for use by Bön shamans as tools in healing and other religious ceremonies. As Bön rituals merged with Buddhist practices, the spiritual tools evolved alongside. Some of the symbols we find on prayer flags today originated with the Bön people. The snow lion, garuda, thunder dragon, and tiger all predate the arrival of Buddhism in Tibet. In the center of these ancient flags would appear the treasured horse, surrounded by the animals.

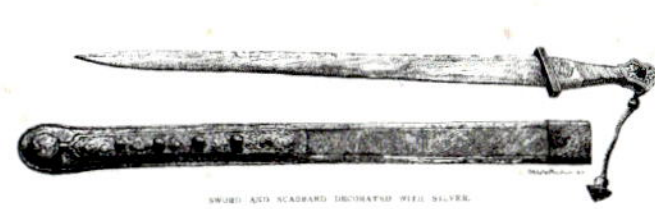

*Banners hoisted during war in ancient Tibet were called Ru-dar. These military flags are thought to be the very first prayer-type flags found in the Himalayan region.*

Tibetans believe that anyone can attain enlightenment, and therefore each person should help others on the path to becoming a Buddha. Prayer flags are a symbol of this wonderful intention: to help ourselves as well as others become more compassionate and open human beings. When we see prayer flags flapping in the breeze, we may feel warm and hopeful, knowing good intentions are being sent out on the wings of air.

*The colors of prayer flags usually appear in the following order from right to left: blue, white, red, green, then yellow.*

## CHAPTER TWO

# BLESSINGS IN THE AIR

## READING AND UNERSTANDING TRADITIONAL PRAYER FLAGS

## GET CLOSER

Take a look at a prayer flag now. Usually prayer flags are printed from wooden blocks onto brightly colored cotton or polyester. Most flags from the Himalayan mountain region are printed on polyester today, as cotton is hard to come by. If you have a string of five flags, each is connected to the others by a strand of rope that runs along the top. These flags can be strung horizontally; imagine hanging them up as you would Christmas lights around an entryway, eave, or window frame. You can also get prayer flags to be hung vertically. Typically the vertical-hanging flags may be larger than the horizontal flags. You can buy your prayer flags preprinted with different symbols for different occasions, or you can buy blank sets to add your own prayers and wishes. In this kit you have both. You can even buy paper prayer flags that can be used as lovely garlands for your home or garden.

## MORE THAN SKIN DEEP

There is symbolic significance to our prayer flags. We won't find pink, turquoise, mauve, sea foam, and baby blue dyed flags to match our décor and our moods. Prayer flags appear in primary blue, white, red, green, and yellow to symbolize the five elements that make up our physical world, and therefore our selves. Each color corresponds with earth, water, fire, air, and wind.

If you investigate prayer flags further, you'll note that some sites list the colors of prayer flags and the corresponding elements differently than others. This depends on the source of your information. For instance, in some schools of Tibetan Buddhism you'll find:

Blue = Space/Sky/Ether/Wind

White = Air/Clouds

Red = Fire

Green = Water

Yellow = Earth

In other schools you'll find that white means water, green means space, and blue means wind.

© Photo by: Erik De Graaf

The five colors can also represent the five directions (north, south, east, west, and center), the five meditation buddhas, or the five wisdoms. The five meditation buddhas can loosely be translated to represent the different aspects of wisdom in an enlightened mind: the qualities of compassion, harmony, mirror-like wisdom, universal kindness, and all-perfecting wisdom.

*May the horse of good fortune run fast and increase the power of life, influence, fortune, wealth, health, and so forth.*

—Bön Mantra

*Lung ta* is the Tibetan word for the horizontal prayer flags and is translated as "wind horse." Horses, symbolically, are fleet of foot, noble, and often historically evoked an aura of royalty.

Traditionally, Tibet was a horse-based, nomadic culture, and horses were valued for their wonderful spirit as well as their practical uses. The wind horse symbolizes an uplifting energy that carries our prayers on the breeze on the fleetest of feet. One of the most commonly found traditional prayer flags features a wind horse in the center. Hanging the flag with the horse facing upwards into the sky allows your prayers to be carried away at great speed on the back of the noble beast.

The Three Jewels in Buddhism represent Buddha (the enlightened one), dharma (his teaching), and sangha (his following, the Buddhist community).

Traditional prayer flags are printed with prayers, mantras, auspicious symbols, and invocations. They are designed to benefit both those who hang them and those who receive the blessings as they carry out over us on the wind. The traditional Buddhist symbols that appear are usually pictorial manifestations of enlightened beings. These beings represent different aspects of the enlightened mind, such as compassion, wisdom, and love. Some of the symbols that might appear as the centralized figure on your traditional prayer flags include the following:

WIND HORSE PRAYER FLAGS: These prayer flags typically show the wind horse centered on the flag with three flaming jewels on its back. This is one of the most common prayer flags and brings uplifting energy and good fortune. In each corner you will find one of the Four Dignitaries and the three main bodhisattvas (see below).

CHENREZIG PRAYER FLAGS: Chenrezig (also known as Avalokiteshvara) is the embodiment of compassion, the Bodhisattva of Compassion. Chenrezig is often depicted holding a lotus or with four arms.

STUPA PRAYER FLAGS: A stupa will be the central figure on these prayer flags. Stupas are holy sites that represent the Buddha and his enlightenment. In Tibet, they are usually dome-shaped with a central spire.

SHAKYAMUNI THANGKA PRAYER FLAGS: Centered on this flag is the Shakyamuni Buddha (the buddha of our time), usually in his earth-touching pose.

MAHAKALA PRAYER FLAGS: Mahakala was originally a demon who was tamed by the bodhisattvas Avalokiteshvara and Manjushri (the bodhisattva of

*A bodhisattva (translated as enlightened being) is one whose sole purpose is to achieve enlightenment so that he or she can save others from suffering. Mother Teresa is a wonderful example of a non-Buddhist bodhisattva. Bodhisattvas are motivated by pure compassion and tender love.*

discriminating, transcendant wisdom) and turned into the fiercest of protectors of the dharma. Mahakala is easily recognizable by this fierce and frightening expression.

© Photo by: Sonia Sorbi

MEDICINE BUDDHA: The Medicine Buddha represents healing and wellness. The Medicine Buddha sits in lotus position with his right hand outstretched, holding a healing plant.

PADMASAMBHAVA PRAYER FLAGS: The central figure on these prayer flags is the man instrumental for bringing Buddhism to Tibet.

TARA PRAYER FLAGS: Tara is the goddess of compassion and wisdom. She is said to have been created from a tear shed by Chenrezig when he beheld the enormous task of relieving the suffering of mankind. She is the great protector.

# LIONS, TIGERS, GARUDA, AND MORE!

Other images you might find on your traditional prayer flags include the four dignitaries and the eight symbols of good fortune.

*The Four Dignitaries*:

The Four Dignitaries are four animals that represent qualities one cultivates on the path to enlightenment. These animals are:

The Tiger representing confidence and air

The Snow Lion representing joy and earth

The Garuda, the mythic bird, representing wisdom and fire

The Thunder (or Sky) Dragon representing power and water

The Four Dignitaries are often depicted together on the same flag or can appear singularly.

## *The Eight Symbols of Good Fortune*

In Tibetan Buddhism there are eight symbols that represent good fortune. These symbols often appear on traditional prayer flags.

The parasol is a symbol of protection and wealth, power, and royalty.

The golden fishes represent transcendent wisdom and the good fortune of being relieved of suffering.

The treasure vase represents fulfillment and prosperity.

The lotus represents mental purity: purification of mind, body, and spirit.

The right-turning conch shell represents the dissemination of the Buddha's teaching.

The endless knot is a wonderful symbol of connection.

The victory sign denotes knowledge and the attainment of happiness, victory over ignorance and negative influences.

The wheel represents the turning of the dharma (the Buddha's teachings).

*The three main bodhisattvas in Tibetan Buddhism are Chenrezig, Manjushri, and Vajrapani, representing the wonderful enlightenment qualities of compassion, wisdom, and power, respectively.*

# Other Symbols on Your Prayer Flags

You might also find any of these symbols (below) on your traditional prayer flags.

## Seven Jewels of Royal Power

- Precious Wheel
- Precious Jewel
- Precious Queen
- Precious Minister
- Precious Elephant
- Precious Horse
- Precious General

The Victory Sign: a symbol of victory over suffering

© Photo by: Jose Fuente

## OM MANI PADME HUM

*A mantra is a mystical incantation whose repetition contains the potential for spiritual connection and transformation. Mantras are also often written on prayer wheels. A sutra is a text based on the teachings of Shakyamuni Buddha.*

Flags might include prayers for good fortune, longevity and good health; sutras, such as the Heart Sutra; and mantras such as the ever-present *om mani pade hum*, the most widely used of all Tibetan mantras. Om made padme hum can be translated as "Come! Jewel in the Lotus! In my heart!" It is used to invoke the spirit of Chenrizeg, the Bhodisattva of Compassion, also known as Avalokiteshvara. The written form of the word often appears on prayer wheels, and spinning the prayer wheel is said to have the same effect.

More modern flags might include prayers written by the current Dalai Lama. You can even buy nontraditional flags, such as the flags inscribed with The Rainbow Bridge poem, for those who have lost a pet. Or the Prayer to Avert War Flag written by Kamala Radza Dvipa (Padgyal Lingpa), which is inscribed with the following prayer: "May the terrible weapons of modern warfare—nuclear weapons, biological weapons, and so forth—that threaten to destroy the Earth, and all our ill fortune leading to great wars and armed conflict, be utterly pacified, and may the world enjoy happiness similar to that of the golden age!"

© Photo by: Rafael Laguillo

## CHAPTER THREE

# ON THE WINGS OF PRAYER

## DISPLAYING YOUR PRAYER FLAGS

Buddha said: "What we think, we become." This is very important to keep in mind when we are preparing and hanging our prayer flags. Whatever our prayer flags say, whatever art and symbols are represented in the colorful display, the intention we have in our hearts when we hang them is everything. Hang your prayer flags with reverence; this is an auspicious occasion. Hold a tender and kind heart, and consider the blessings you are about to put on the wind to be carried to the far reaches of the world.

© Photo by: Melissa Schalke

# SUGGESTIONS FOR HANGING PRAYER FLAGS

According to Tibetan tradition, there are auspicious and inauspicious days for the hanging of prayer flags. You can check out Lama Yeshe's Wisdom Archive on the web at
*http://www.lamayeshe.com/lamazopa/prayer_flags.shtml*
for a list of such dates and an explanation of traditional Tibetan thought on the hanging of prayer flags.

The New Year is the most auspicious time to hang your prayer flags, but generally any new beginning is just as good: a new season, a wedding, a birth, a new business venture, et cetera. Prayer flags can also be hung for funerals and to help one cope with grief. Keep in mind that when we hang our prayer flags we are hanging them for the well-being of others. As you hang prayer flags after a loss, you should hang them for the good fortune of your lost one as well as all those who have gone before.

Photo by: Melissa Schalke

## HANG THEM HIGH

Prayer flags are traditionally flown on high places, such as mountain summits, rooftops, temple roofs, eaves, from high trees, and spires. If you view photos of prayer flags in Nepal and Tibet, you will see that multiple flags are hung in a powerful confusion of color, texture, and spirit. New flags are hung alongside older flags, and the brightness of the new contrast starkly with the faded tatters of the old.

You can hang flags from rooftop, between trees, on the porch, or erect a wooden pole in the middle of the yard and string the flags from the top of the pole down and out to the bottom, creating a maypole effect. According to Timothy Clark in his informative article, bamboo is highly recommended for prayer flag flagpoles.

You can hang flags indoors in a meditation space or sacred area of the house. Remember to hang the flags in the correct order: blue, white, red, green, and yellow. If you have prayer flags to be hung vertically, blue goes at the top. From left to right, blue usually comes first.

You can gather the entire family together for a flag-hanging day. Invite your neighbors and friends.

Hang your flags for peace for all mankind, wishing to all who suffer that they should have harmony, abundance, longevity, health, and happiness. Send your blessing out on the wind, where they will reach faraway people who suffer from the ravages of war, starvation, unrest, drought, poverty, and illness. Tibetans often burn incense when hanging prayer flags, so you can add to the occasion with pots of aromatic incense burning around the chosen sites.

As Geshe Rabten says in *Advice from a Spiritual Friend,* "The correct motivation for every action is essential." And so we must be emotionally and spiritually prepared for the hanging of our flags. It is a sacred act to string up a set of prayer flags, and the only wrong way to hang your prayer flags would be without respect and proper intention in your heart. What an act of generosity it is to send out your blessings to the far corners of the earth for the benefit of all sentient beings! How tragic to do so with a dark heart. Please hang your prayer flags with the reverence and good-natured light-heartedness they—and everyone—deserves. Naturally, we should honor the things of this world, tending them so that they last. We should avoid getting caught up in patterns of endless over-consumption. Direct your self to cultivate the compassion, good will, and love that will imbue these symbols with carefully nurtured positive attributes.

© Photo by: Wang Sanjun

## MAKING YOUR OWN PRAYER FLAGS

Included in this kit is a set of blank prayer flags so that you can create your own prayers, mantras, and blessings. However, you can make additional prayers flags out of materials you have at home. You can use colorful pieces of paper, newspaper, or cloth for the flag and decorate with stamped art, illustrations, paintings, clippings from magazines and newspapers. Use colorful cotton fabric that will stand up to the elements for longer lasting flags. Stamp with printing blocks for homemade designs with animal, leaf, or flower motifs, or use vibrant fabric paints. You can embroider your flag with traditional symbols or those of your own design.

Leave enough space at the top of each flag so that you can run twine or rope across the flags horizontally for hanging. Staple, glue, tape, or sew the string to the flags securely. Chapter 4 has suggestions for prayers and mantras for your homemade blessing flags. Employ the entire family in the making and stringing of your prayer flags. It creates a lovely atmosphere of peace and joy in your home, and children love the bright colors and wonderful textures of prayer flags. It's a fun group activity and a terrific way to teach the kids about generosity of spirit, compassion for themselves and others, and the connectivity of all sentient beings.

*Tibetan Buddhists would prefer that you not use your flags to decorate clothing or convert into fashion items such as scarves and skirts. Treat your prayer flags with the reverence they deserve. Do not put them on the ground or walk on them. Treat them kindly and with great care.*

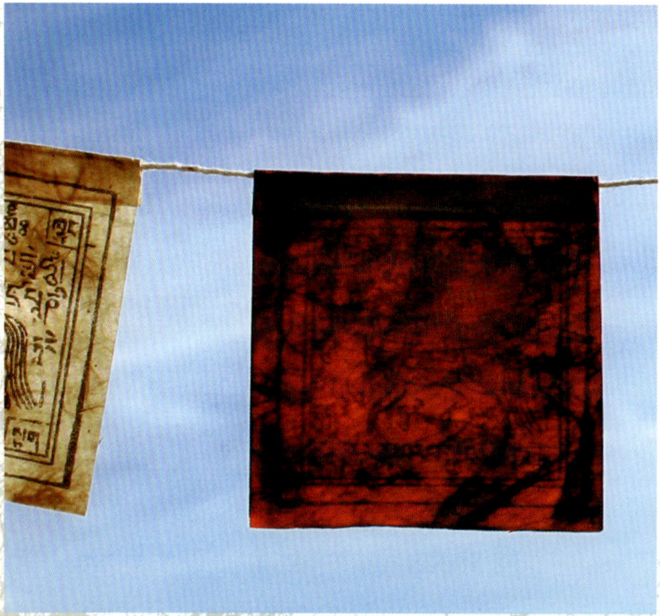

© Photo by: Sonia Sorbi

# DISPOSING OF YOUR PRAYER FLAGS

Prayer flags remind us of the impermanence of all things. They are not meant to last forever, but will fade and disintegrate over time as Mother Nature wears them away. Soon enough you will have a washed out string of tattered fabric hanging over your garden. The prayer flags have done their job. You can either discard the prayer flags in a respectful fashion or you can leave them to the elements until they are no longer visible.

Please do not discard your prayer flags in the garbage, but treat them with respect. Follow through on the cycle of life and return them to the universe by burning them. Scatter the ashes to the wind so that the very last vestiges of your blessings and prayer can be dispersed across the earth for the benefit of all.

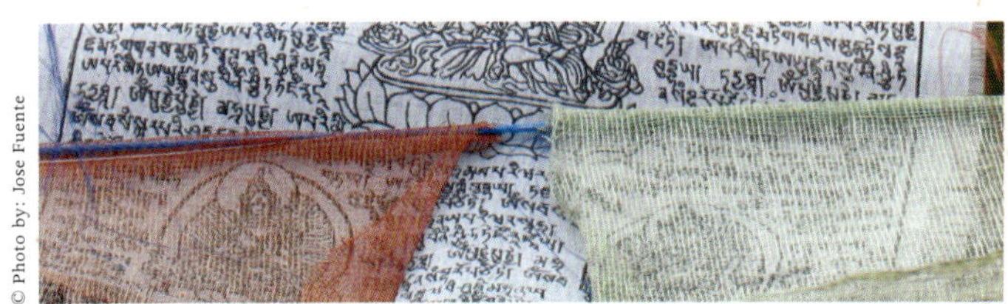

# KILL THE BUDDHA

We all hold images and ideals we believe are sacred. Unfortunately, these images and ideals only hinder us. There is an old Buddhist saying that tells us, "If you meet the Buddha, kill the Buddha." Shakyamuni Buddha taught us that we are all buddhas, we just haven't realized it yet. We think there is a door shut against us, but we are the ones holding the door closed, afraid to open it. If we are buddhas ourselves, then if we encounter anything separate from ourselves, we must kill the buddha—we must kill the separation that exists between us and anything else.

Mentors are invaluable in this process. Learning from those who have already walked the path is instrumental in our awakening. However, we often chase teachers, hoping to soak up what they have, believing they are somehow better than we are. We move from teacher to teacher, finding the sacred everywhere but within. In this regard, Shakyamuni Buddha taught us that nothing is sacred and everything is sacred. Killing the Buddha means we erase the fantasy we have about other people and other things, and become our own lamp lighting the way. Treat your prayer flags with respect, but don't mistake the messenger for the message.

© Photo by: Ron Sumners

## CHAPTER FOUR

# YOUR OPEN HEART

## CREATING YOUR OWN PRAYERS AND MANTRAS

Traditional prayer flags are like old friends. I was recently on an early spring walk down a riverside trail with my yellow lab, Roscoe, when I noticed a string of small prayer flags hung between two trees in a garden overlooking the river. The garden was still scruffy and bare from the long winter, but the red, white, blue, yellow and green flags fluttered cheerfully in the moving air. Immediately I felt a sense of kinship with the property owners, who had a Buddha statue set beneath the prayer flags. I wondered what was in their hearts as they strung up their flags.

© Photo by: Rich Bartell

*"Becoming aware of intention is a key to awakening in moment-to-moment practice. In each situation that calls for our engagement, some inner intention will precede our response. Buddhist psychology teaches that intention is what makes the pattern of our karma."*

—JACK KORNFIELD, *After the Ecstasy, the Laundry*

## THE ARTIST WITHIN

With this book you have a set of blank prayer flags, which you can decorate in any way you choose. You can draw an animal in the center, such as a horse—as on traditional flags—or create something entirely new. You can borrow from other cultures. Animals have different symbolic meanings depending on the source. For instance, below are some Native American animal symbols and their meanings:

BEAR: *power, healer, strength*

BUFFALO: *life builder*

BUTTERFLY: *change, transformation*

COYOTE: *humor*

DEER: *Love, kindness, gracefulness and sensitivity*

DRAGONFLY: *carefree, activity*

EAGLE: *protector from evil*

FOX: *intuitive, resourceful*

OWL: *wisdom*

SNAKE: *life, death, and rebirth*

TURTLE: *long, beautiful life*

WOLF: *teacher*

Perhaps an animal has a personal significance for you: Maybe a dog symbolizes loyalty or a cat, independence. A bird might mean freedom, a butterfly grace. A dove commonly symbolizes peace and is a lovely sign for our troubled times.

You are certainly not limited to animals, however. There are so many symbols of significance the world over. You can use ancient symbols such as labyrinths and crosses; you can use cornucopias, altars, stars, flowers, zodiac signs, nature signs (clouds, earth, fire, rain, sea, sun), insects, stones, food, plants, trees, and so on.

You can write your own prayers, wishes, hopes, and dreams on your prayer flags as well. You can decorate each flag differently to tell a progressive story. You can use your flags for times of transition or times of celebration. Here are some ideas for the use of your prayer flags:

## WEDDINGS

You can marry in front of your garden, at the foot of a tree that you might have planted yourself. You can string traditional prayer flags all around the garden, knowing they will carry your intentions to live a long and harmonious life together out into the breeze and beyond. You can use the write-able flags to enhance your wedding or another's by inscribing meaningful words. What a thoughtful shower gift for a friend or family member! You can inscribe any of the following on your flags:

- *Wedding vows*
- *Hopes for the future*
- *Promises for the future: for example, patience, kindness, compassion, loyalty, steadfastness*
- *Poetry*
- *Song lyrics*
- *Prayers*

# BIRTHS

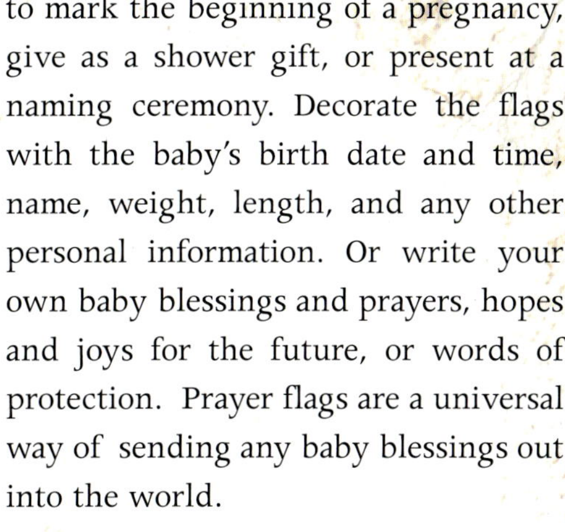

Personalized prayer flags also make a wonderful way to mark the beginning of a pregnancy, give as a shower gift, or present at a naming ceremony. Decorate the flags with the baby's birth date and time, name, weight, length, and any other personal information. Or write your own baby blessings and prayers, hopes and joys for the future, or words of protection. Prayer flags are a universal way of sending any baby blessings out into the world.

© Photo by: Ra Khalil

HIMALAYAN STORE & EXPORTS
SAKURA
桜

## TRANSITIONS

In times of transition and uncertainty, prayer flags can bring comfort to our hearts and our homes. When we move to a new home, hanging prayer flags can be a wonderful way to bless our new space and send harmonious intention into our new neighorhood.

Opening a new business venture is also a momentous occasion. Hanging prayer flags at this time will center you with a gesture of goodwill, hope, and intended integrity, enabling you to launch your business with great promise. How lovely to welcome a new beginning with an open heart!

# Loss of Loved Ones

When a loved one dies, we are overcome with grief, loss, and uncertainty. Prayer flags can help us to send our lost ones out onto the breeze with prayers and wishes for eternal comfort and freedom. Hanging prayer flags while grieving gives us the chance to gather our thoughts about what we have had. Our grief is often in proportion to the love we have experienced: The larger the grief, the greater the love. Prayer flags can help us to see how fortunate we have been to have such love in our lives. The actual hanging of the flags can bring the family together, whether you have lost a family member, friend, or much-loved pet.

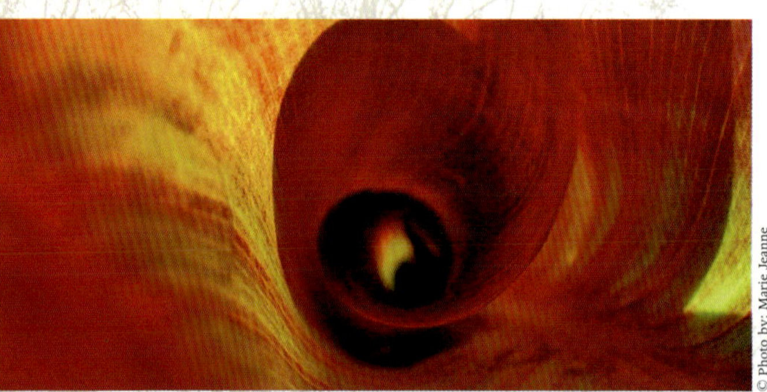

© Photo by: Marie Jeanne

## WAR

In times of strife anywhere in the world—be it in your own home or abroad–you can hang prayer flags for peace. On his recent tour of the U.S., the Dalai Lama reminded us that peace is a universal responsibility and must start in our own hearts and minds. Hanging prayer flags is an outward action we can take to express the inner peace we desire. Just as the state of the world affects us, we affect the state of the world. Everything is interconnected and we must do our part to realize peace and harmony in our towns, in our homes, in ourselves.

There are so many different occasions for you to create and hang your prayer flags. Your creativity and open heart will help you find the right words for any occasion, whether you decided on traditional flags or creating personalized flags.

CHAPTER FIVE

# SAGE WORDS

## WISDOM AND AFFIRMATIONS FOR YOUR PRAYER FLAGS

You can call on the sagacity of others for your blank prayer flags. This chapter contains some wonderful words of wisdom from which you can draw. In the true spirit of Buddhism—which encourages joining everyone together in harmony—you can borrow wisdom from all walks of life. We are not limited to the sayings of Bodhidharma, the Dalai Lama, or Buddhist teachers like Shantideva or Chögyam Trungpa , though they do have wise things to impart to us. Writers, spiritual leaders, poets, artists, and politicians have all passed on words that have deeply affected us and changed the way we think about things. Over the years, I have found that two of the most powerful words of all are "thank you."

Pick from some of the moving and thought-provoking treasures below, and remember: It's your intention that truly makes a difference.

## COMPASSION/KINDNESS

Fill your mind
with compassion.

—Buddha

*The best portion of a good man's life: his little, nameless, unremembered acts of kindness and love.* —William Wordsworth

Kindness in words creates confidence.
Kindness in thinking creates profoundness.
Kindness in giving creates love. —Lao-Tzu

# *Life is an adventure in forgiveness.*

—Norman Cousins

Kind words can be short and easy to speak but their echoes are truly endless.

—Mother Teresa

© Photo by: Øystein Litleskare

Three things in human life are important. The first is to be kind. The second is to be kind. The third is to be kind.

—Henry James

© Photo by: Adrian Hughes

This is my simple religion. There is no need for temples; no need for complicated philosophy. Our own brain, our own heart is our temple; the philosophy is kindness.

—His Holiness, the 14th Dalai Lama

Compassion… cannot be considered complete by merely feeling the suffering of another as one's own. Compassion must be accompanied by action. Compassion is a behavior, not just a thought.

— ALAN CLEMENTS, *Instinct For Freedom*

© Photo by: Vadim Kozlovsky

Deeds of kindness are equal in weight to all the commandments.

—THE TALMUD

Wherever there is a human being, there is a chance for a kindness. —SENECA

# GRATITUDE

If the only prayer you said in your whole life was "thank you," that would suffice. —MEISTER ECKHART

*As we express our gratitude,*
*we must never forget that*
*the highest appreciation is*
*not to utter words,*
*but to live by them.*

—JOHN FITZGERALD KENNEDY

WHEN EATING A FRUIT,
THINK OF THE PERSON
WHO PLANTED THE TREE.

—*Vietnamese saying*

Whatever I am
offered in devotion
with a pure heart—
a leaf, a flower,
fruit, or water—
I accept with joy.

—BHAGAVAD GITA

# LIVING WELL

Manifest plainness,
Embrace simplicity,
Reduce selfishness,
Have few desires.

—LAO-TZU, TAO TE CHING

## Live simply that others might simply live.

—ELIZABETH SEATON

*May I be the doctor and the medicine,*
*And may I be the nurse*
*For all such beings in the world*
*Until everyone is healed.*
—Shantideva's Bodhisattva

© Photo By: Jonathan Lewis

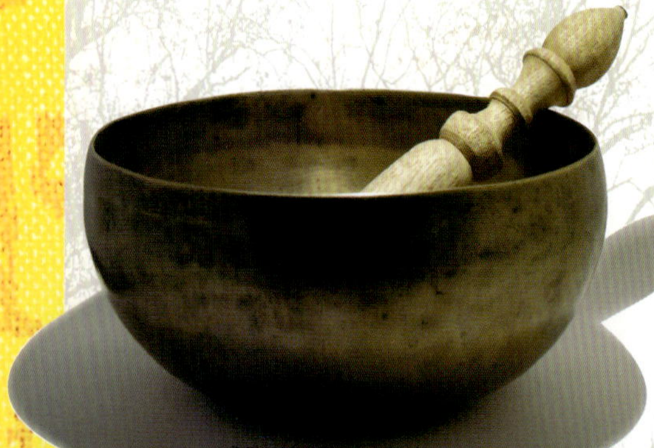

## Vow Who is rich? He who rejoices in his portion.

—THE TALMUD

There are two ways to live your life. One is as though nothing is a miracle. The other is as though everything is a miracle.

—Albert Einstein

If you find one thing boring, you will find everything boring.

—Dogen

I feel no need for any other faith than my faith in the kindness of human beings. I am so absorbed in the wonder of earth and the life upon it that I cannot think of heaven and angels.

— Pearl S. Buck

© Photo by: Marilyn Barbone

*If* you have attachment to your self-interest,
You do not have the spirit of enlightenment.
If grasping arises, You do not have the
authentic View…

—MANJUSHRI'S REVELATION TO SACHEN KUNGA NYINGPO

In the beginner's mind there are many possibilities, but in the expert's mind, there are few.

—SHUNRYU SUZUKI

## And the greatest of these is love.

—St. Paul

© Photo by: Cecilia Lim

# The 10 Grave Precepts as noted by John Daido Loori in *Invoking Reality*

Affirm Life

Be Giving

Honor the Body

Manifest Truth

Proceed Clearly (Clear Mind)

See the Perfection

Realize Self and Other as One

Give Generously

Actualize Harmony

Experience the Intimacy of Things

Om Madi Pade Hum

—TIBETAN MANTRA

© Photo by: Gina Smith

There are no doors to the hells;
you yourself make the doors.

—HSUAN HUA

*Nobody sees a flower, really—
it is so small we haven't time,
and to see takes time.*

—GEORGIA O'KEEFE

MAY THE HORSE OF GOOD FORTUNE RUN FAST AND INCREASE THE POWER OF LIFE, INFLUENCE, FORTUNE, WEALTH, HEALTH, AND SO FORTH.

—*Bon mantra*

Everything we do is an act of poetry or a painting if we do it with mindfulness.

—THICH NHAT HANH

*Who wrote this play in which we have to laugh, cry, and exit according to the script? No god can write it, nor can Buddha. Only your own mind can write it.*

—JAE WOONG

Simplicity, simplicity, simplicity!

—*Henry David Thoreau*

We are the leaves of one branch, the drops of one sea, the flowers of one garden.

—JEAN BAPTISTE HENRY LACORDAIRE

*To live only for some future goal is shallow. It's the sides of the mountain that sustain life, not the top.*

—ROBERT M. PIRSIG

The obstacle is the path.

—ZEN PROVERB

Be content with what you have, rejoice in the way things are. When you realize there is nothing lacking, the whole world belongs to you. —LAO TZU

We are cups, constantly and quietly being filled. The trick is, knowing how to tip ourselves over and let the beautiful stuff out. —RAY BRADBURY

If you understand, things are just as they are; if you do not understand, things are just as they are.

—BUDDHIST PROVERB

To study Buddhism is to study the Self. To study the Self is to forget the Self and To forget the Self is to be enlightened by the Ten Thousand Things. —DOGEN

# PEACE

© Photo by: Elena Ray

*Nonviolence does not mean nonaction. Nonviolence means we act with love and compassion. The moment we stop acting, we undermine the principle of nonviolence.*

—*Thich Nhat Hang, Be Still and Know*

*Grant me the serenity to accept the things I cannot change, Courage to change the things I can, And wisdom to know the difference.*

—The Serenity Prayer

Victory produces hostility, because the ones who are defeated live in grief. Letting go of victory and defeat, The tranquil mind lives in happiness.

—The Dhammapada

*People say "I want peace." If you remove I (ego), and your want (desire), you are left with peace. We can never obtain peace in the world if we neglect the inner world and don't make peace with ourselves. World Peace must develop out of inner peace.* —HIS HOLINESS, THE 14TH DALAI LAMA

TO WIN A WAR IS AS DISASTROUS AS TO LOSE ONE.

—AGATHA CHRISTIE

*You can't shake hands with a clenched fist.*

—INDIRA GANDHI

When the power of love overcomes the love of power the world will know peace. —JIMI HENDRIX

*Sentient beings are numberless. I vow to save them.*
*Desires are inexhaustible. I vow to put an end to them.*
*The Dharmas are boundless. I vow to master them.*
*The enlightened way is unattainable. I vow to attain it.*

—THE FOUR GREAT VOWS

## LOVE/FRIENDSHIP

Where there is great love,
there are always miracles.

—*Willa Cather*

*Not by hate is hate defeated; hate is quenched by love.*

—DHAMMAPADA

THE FAMILY STANDS TOGETHER LIKE A FOREST,
WHILE THE STORMS BLOW DOWN THE TREE THAT STANDS ALONE.

—JATAKA 74

*You cannot be friends upon any other terms than upon the terms of equality.* —*Woodrow Wilson*

Love *is* the master key that opens the gates *of* happiness.

—OLIVER WENDELL HOLMES

UNLESS WE PRACTICE LOVING FEELINGS TOWARD EVERYONE WE MEET, DAY IN, DAY OUT, WE'RE MISSING OUT ON THE MOST JOYOUS PART OF LIFE. IF WE CAN ACTUALLY OPEN OUR HEARTS, THERE'S NO DIFFICULTY IN BEING HAPPY.

—AYYA KHEMA

*To love oneself is the beginning of a life-long romance.* —Oscar Wilde

Many waters cannot quench love, neither can the floods drown it.

—Song of Solomon

Love *conquers all things: let us too give in to* Love.

–*Virgil Eclogues*

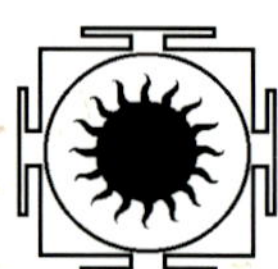

LOVE COMFORTETH LIKE SUNSHINE AFTER RAIN.

—William Shakespeare

When you get right down to it, the secret of having it all is loving it all.

—*Dr. Joyce Brothers*

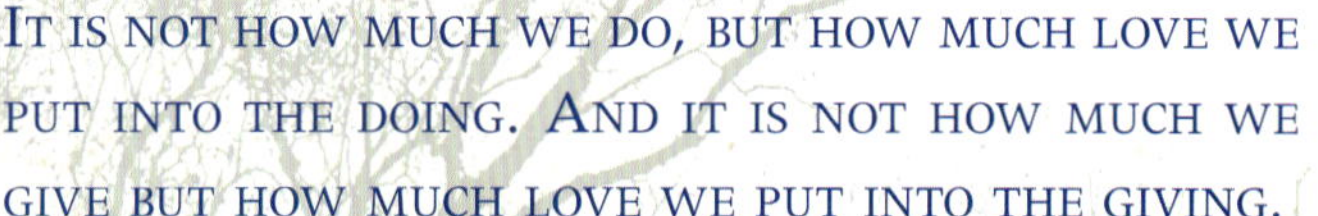

It is not how much we do, but how much love we put into the doing. And it is not how much we give but how much love we put into the giving.

—Mother Teresa

# PATIENCE

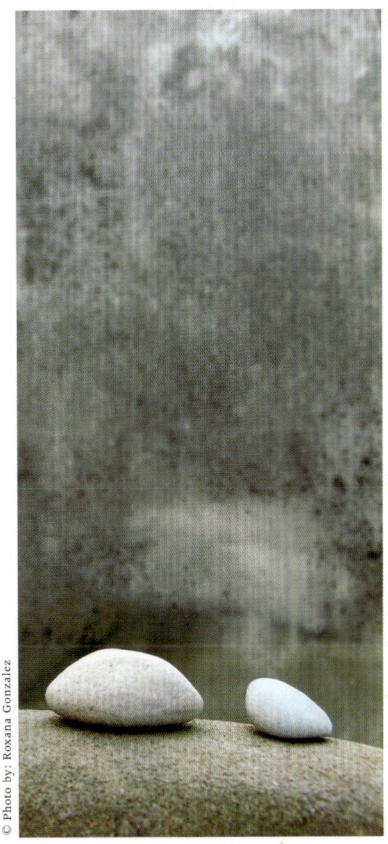

© Photo by: Roxana Gonzalez

Nothing worthwhile
is achieved overnight.

—Bhante Henepola Gunaratana,
*Mindfulness in Plain English*

Our real *blessings* often
appear to us in the shapes
of pains, losses and
disappointments; but let us
have *patience,* and we soon
shall see them in their
proper figures. —Joseph Addison

In the struggle between
the stone and the water,
in time, the water wins.

—Chinese proverb

*If you are* ***patient***
*in one moment of anger,*
*you will escape a hundred*
*days of sorrow*

—Unknown

*Just as a person*
*who has been gone for a long time*
*is welcomed on his safe return home with joy*
*by his relatives,*
*friends,*
*and well-wishers,*
*So will you be welcomed,*
*when you move beyond this life,*
*by the good deeds you have done*
*in this lifetime.*

—The Dhammapada



THIS BEING HUMAN
IS A GUEST HOUSE.

—Rumi

*Seeing death as the end of life is like seeing the horizon as the end of the ocean.*

—David Searls

Memory is, more indelible than ink.

—Anita Loos, *Kiss Hollywood Goodbye*

*Others may forget you,*
*but not I.*
*I am haunted*
*by your beautiful ghost.*

—UNTITLED, *One Hundred Poems from the Japanese, 1964, Kenneth Rexroth, tr.*

The truth you believe and cling to makes you unavailable to hear anything new. —PEMA CHODRON

*Go, return each to her mother's house....*

—RUTH 1:8

*Let us not look back in anger or forward in fear, but around in awareness.*

—James Thurber

If you want others to be happy, practice compassion. If you want to be happy, practice compassion

—His Holiness, the 14th The Dalai Lama

"Only in solitude do we find ourselves; and in finding ourselves, we find in ourselves all our brothers in solitude."

—*Miguel de Unanimo*

*In the midst of winter, I discovered that there was in me an invincible summer.*

–Albert Camus

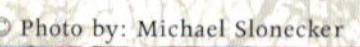

© Photo by: Michael Slonecker

We must free ourselves of the hope that the sea will ever rest. We must learn to sail in high winds.

—Hanmer Parsons Grant

*Joy can be real only if people look upon their life as a service, and have a definite object in life outside themselves and their personal happiness.* —Leo Tolstoy

Happiness is, more a matter of subtraction than addition.

— Meister Eckhart

*"If I thought I could find God in a Himalayan Cave, I would proceed there immediately; but I know I cannot find him apart from humanity."*

—Mahatma Gandhi,
*My Experiments With Truth*

*Of all the rights of women, the greatest is to be a mother.* —Lin Yutang

Mother's arms are made of tenderness, and sweet sleep blesses the child who lies therein.

—Victor Hugo

The love that moves the sun and other stars

—Dante Alighieri

I think my life began with waking up and loving my mother's face.

—George Eliot

The moment a child is born, the mother is also born. —Rajneesh

Neither fire
nor wind, birth
nor death
can erase
our good deeds.

—Buddha

# RIGHT ACTION

WITH EVERY DEED, YOU ARE SOWING A SEED,
THOUGH THE HARVEST YOU MAY NOT SEE.

—ELLA WHEELER WILCOX

*Life's most urgent question is: what are you doing for others?*

—MARTIN LUTHER KING, JR.

The problem in my life and other people's lives is not the absence of knowing what to do, but the absence of doing it.

—PETER DRUCKER

"You must be the change you wish to see in the world."

—MAHATMA GANDHI

*Action springs not from thought, but from a readiness for responsibility.*

—DIETRICH BONHOEFFER

Mistakes are the portals of discovery.

—JAMES JOYCE

*It is one of the most beautiful compensations of this life that no man can sincerely try to help another without helping himself.* — RALPH WALDO EMERSON

THE CONSTITUTION ONLY GIVES PEOPLE THE RIGHT TO PURSUE HAPPINESS. YOU HAVE TO CATCH IT YOURSELF.

—BEN FRANKLIN

THERE HAS NEVER BEEN AN ENLIGHTENED PERSON. THERE ARE ONLY ENLIGHTENED ACTIVITIES.

—BODHIN KJOLHEDE

© Photo by: Marilyn Barbone

*And remember, as Buddha reminds us, "There is only one time that it is essential to awaken. That time is now."*

# APPENDICES

Sources for Purchasing Additional Prayer Flags:

The following websites are suggested for their abundant selection of prayer flags. Some of the flags on these sites are unusual and worth checking out! There are many other wonderful places to purchase prayer flags, so make sure you shop around and find what feels right for your needs.

Cider Mill Press: www.cidermillpress.com

Dharma Shop: www.dharmashop.com

Four Gates: http://www.fourgates.com/flags.asp

Hither and Yon:
http://www.hitherandyononline.com/Prayerflags/prayerflags.htm

Mountain Valley Center:
http://www.mountainvalleycenter.com/store/html/prayertools.htm

Tibetan Prayer Flags and Banners from Radiant Heart: www.prayerflags.com

West Wind Collection: http://www.westwindcollection.com/

# BIBLIOGRAPHY

Books:

Dagyab Rinpoche, *Buddhist Symbols in Tibetan Culture* (Wisdom Publications, MA 1995).

Edited by Josh Bartok, *Daily Wisdom: 365 Buddhist Inspirations* (Wisdom Publications, MA, 2001).

Hanh, Thich Nhat, *Be Still and Know* (Riverhead Books, NY, NY, 1996).

His Holiness the Dalai Lama, *The Dalai Lama's Little Book of Wisdom* (HarperCollins, London, 2002).

Kornfield, Jack, *After the Ecstasy, the Laundry* (Bantam Books, NY, NY, 2001).

Larkin, Geri, *The Still Point Dhammapada: Living the Buddha's Essential Teachings* (Harper San Francisco, CA, 2003).

Loori, John Daido, *Invoking Reality* ( Dharma Communications, Mt. Tremper, NY, 1998).

Rahula, Walpola, *What the Buddha Taught* (Grove Press, NY, 1959).

# WEBSITES:

AAA Native American Arts @ www.aaanativeamericanarts.com
Buddha Nature @ http://www.buddhanature.com/
Lama Yeshe Wisdom Archive @
http://www.lamayeshe.com/lamazopa/prayer_flags.shtml
Metareligion @ http://www.meta-religion.com
Saraswati Bhawan Articles @
http://www.saraswatibhawan.org/pub_art_PrayerFlagTrad.htm See: "The Prayer Flag Tradition" by Timothy Clark
Tibetan Prayer Flags @ http://www.tibetanprayerflag.com/history.html
Tibetan Prayer Flags and Banners from Radiant Heart @ http://www.prayerflags.com/
Tibetan Treasures @ http://www.tibetantreasures.com
Yoniversum.nl @ http://www.yoniversum.nl/dakini/dirtib5.html

# ABOUT CIDER MILL PRESS BOOK PUBLISHERS

*Good ideas ripen with time. From seed to harvest, Cider Mill Press strives to bring fine reading, information, and entertainment together between the covers of its creatively crafted books. Our Cider Mill bears fruit twice a year, publishing a new crop of titles each Spring and Fall.*


Visit us on the web at
www.cidermillpress.com
or write to us at
12 Port Farm Road
Kennebunkport, Maine 04046

Where Good Books
are Ready for Press